Date Due

5-27-8			
MAR 04 '8			
MAR 24 '8			
OCT 11 '83			
Oct. 3 83			
OCT 31 '83			
NOV 18 8			

SPACE
TECHNOLOGY
SPINOFFS

SPACE TECHNOLOGY SPINOFFS

BY GENE GURNEY

FRANKLIN WATTS
NEW YORK | LONDON | 1979
AN !MPACT BOOK

Photographs courtesy of:
National Aeronautics and Space Administration.

Library of Congress Cataloging in Publication Data

Gurney, Gene.
Space technology spinoffs.

(An Impact book)
Bibliography: p.
Includes index.
SUMMARY: Discusses benefits derived from the
NASA space program in areas including medicine,
environmental protection, energy conservation, and
transportation.
1. Technology transfer—Juvenile literature. 2. As-
tronautics—Juvenile literature. [1. Technology trans-
fer. 2. Astronautics] I. Title.
T174.3.G87   ~~600~~ 609   78-21617
ISBN 0-531-02290-0

CONTENTS

ACKNOWLEDGMENTS

The author and the publisher are indebted to the following people for their help with this book: Ken Senstad and Margaret Ware of NASA Headquarters; James Haggerty, NASA contract writer; the Public Affairs Officers at the NASA Centers, and foremost among the commercial and industrial users of NASA spinoffs, Laura Schmuhl of the General Electric Company's Public Affairs Office at Valley Forge, Pennsylvania.

THE ORIGIN OF SPINOFFS—NASA

In the summer of 1977 the National Aeronautics and Space Administration (NASA) launched two Voyager spacecraft on a journey to infinity. That's right—infinity. The automated probes will explore the great planets Jupiter and Saturn, and then eventually depart the solar system to cruise through outer space for millions of years. Each spacecraft carries a recording of spoken messages in sixty languages, scores of electronic pictures, musical selections and other earth sounds, in the hope that the Voyagers will be intercepted by some extraterrestrial civilization now or sometime in the future.

The Voyager spacecraft is a milestone in NASA's system of planetary exploration. It places greater emphasis on investigation of our solar system's outer planets—Jupiter, Saturn, Uranus, Neptune, and Pluto—along with further probing of the inner planets—Mercury, Venus, Earth, and

Mars. From flight missions like Voyager and from other observations, past, present, and future, NASA is assembling millions of individual bits of cosmic data into a vast informational panorama. The ultimate goal is an understanding of the origin, evolution, and intricate workings of the solar system and its individual planets, and their relationship to earth.

Our earlier probes are already there in outer space. More than 1,000,000,000 miles from earth, a tiny speck in the vast void of space, Pioneer Jupiter flies on. It left its home planet, earth, years ago, never to return. In 1973, the little spacecraft completed its primary mission, passing near the planet Jupiter and sending back photos and technical data. Then it continued onward. Ten years more and it will escape our solar system, the first manmade object to do so.

A year behind Pioneer Jupiter is a companion craft, Pioneer Saturn, which will reach the orbit of the great ringed planet in 1979.

These two interplanetary probes and the two Voyager spacecraft, along with a Viking Mars spacecraft, point up the extraordinary scientific miracles humanity has achieved in its efforts to uncover the mysteries of the universe. They are part of the United States' broad space science plan, which employs deep space probes like the Pioneers, planetary landers like the Viking, and earth-orbiting satellites, nonorbiting sounding rockets, aircraft, balloons and earth-based telescopes in a sweeping study of space phenomena.

In addition to the manned landings on the moon and the unmanned explorations on Mars, American spaceships have flown by Mercury, Venus, and Jupiter—returning data that provides greater understanding of those planets. NASA launched more than three hundred spacecraft into earth orbit or into deep space trajectories. They have mapped the highly complex magnetosphere that extends many thousands of miles from earth, reported on the effects of solar radiation on the earth's ionosphere and its atmosphere, studied the moon, the sun, and the solar wind, and looked far into space, acquiring information on ultraviolet, infrared, X-ray, and gamma-ray radiations, which tell us more about our stars and the outer galaxies. In less than two decades, we probably have learned as much about the universe and our place in it as in all the prior years of history. Yet, the job is just beginning. Exploring the incredibly complex workings of the solar system and the space beyond is a monumental task which, like the universe, has no apparent end. Earlier space probes have provided a solid base for continuing expansion of scientific knowledge, and advancing technology is making available ever more sophisticated spacecraft and instrumentation. The space science plan is far too broad to describe in detail, but a representative sampling of scheduled and contemplated projects includes: continuing study by earth-orbiting satellites of the earth, the sun, and deep space phenomena; a moon-orbiting spacecraft to survey chemical and physical properties of the moon; missions to Venus, Jupiter, and Mars; and manned experiments in space made possible by the advent of the space shuttle in the 1980s, including placing a space telescope in earth orbit.

Scientists, with these and other spacecraft, will add millions of new pieces of knowledge to the rapidly growing parts of the puzzle that is our picture of the universe. All these investigations of mysterious other worlds tell us more and more about the earth's terrestrial sciences, such as meterology, geology, and biology. For the first time in history, the findings of these sciences can be compared with conditions on other planets. This wealth of scientific information is primarily for the use in space exploration but also is of benefit to humanity in the form of technological spinoffs.

These studies of the whole solar system offer better insight into earth's own complex workings. Comparative knowledge of planetary meterology, for instance, would lead to better forecasting of the weather on earth. Greater information about the solar system's geology could make possible precise earthquake predictions. Discoveries about the development of living organisms—or even their lack of development—elsewhere in the universe might spark biological breakthroughs of tremendous significance. Or, when enough pieces of the cosmic puzzle have been fitted together, there will come vast benefits totally unimaginable to us today. We may even receive an audio and/or visual response from outer space to our Jupiter or Voyager probes. This is not such a remote possibility.

Planetary exploration is but one part of NASA's comprehensive and carefully planned space science plan. The agency is also conducting extensive investigation of earth, its atmosphere, its moon, near-earth space, the sun, and the stars of our galaxy and those beyond. In life science research, NASA is studying the effects of the space environment on human and other organisms. Satellites and deep space probes are the most familiar tools of this broad effort but NASA also employs nonorbiting sounding rockets, instrumented aircraft and balloons, optical and radio telescopes, and a great variety of earth-based equipment.

The goals of space science are many, but they have a common denominator—learning more about our planet, earth. Through exploration of the other bodies in the heavens, we are establishing a comparative base for our per-

Solar heating units were first developed for spacecraft.

ceptions of earth, limited until now because, as one scientist put it, "we have been stuck on one planet." By comparing the characteristics of the other planets with those of the earth, we are gaining a new perspective about our own habitat. Greater understanding of the complex forces that control the earth will bring the ability to manage them for broad and sweeping benefit to humankind in the form of space technology spinoffs in our everyday lives.

The NASA Lyndon B. Johnson Space Center at Houston, Texas, is directing the development of the space shuttle which is rocket-launched like earlier spacecraft but with a big difference. Its two solid boosters are recoverable for reuse. The Orbiter, the manned segment of the space shuttle, will operate in space as a piloted, maneuverable vehicle, then return to earth with an aircraftlike landing. When the space shuttle system is totally operational in the 1980s, there will be four Orbiters operating from Kennedy Space Center in Florida and from Vandenberg Air Force Base in California.

Exciting new tasks previously considered impractical or overcostly will become feasible with the space shuttle. It will permit scientists to study and experiment at vantage points as high as 500 miles (804.6 km) above earth. They can perform experiments, study the heavens from a vantage point in space, away from the contaminated atmosphere, or relay information about weather, agricultural, and environmental conditions on earth. The shuttle can open the door to building large structures in space. It can pave the way for "on-orbit" manufacturing in space of certain items, such as pharmaceuticals and crystals for electronics, which are better produced in a vacuum or weightless environment, and for the assembly of habitable space settlements from shuttle-delivered "building blocks." Also, a potential benefit of sweeping dimension is a network of shuttle-erected, orbiting power stations capable of converting the sun's energy into unlimited supplies of electricity for earth use.

In 1977 and 1978, the Orbiter was tested as an atmospheric vehicle at NASA's Dryden Flight Research Center in California. Mounted piggyback atop a modified Boeing 747 jetliner, the Orbiter was carried to altitude and then released in a series of unpowered flights to check out aerodynamic and flight-control characteristics. It then glided to successful landings at the Mojave Desert test area next to the Dryden center.

NASA's Kennedy Space Center in Florida, launch site for the Mercury and Gemini space shots, and the Apollo moon flights and subsequent manned missions, is again humming with activity. A new era has its beginnings in 1979 and 1980 with the first earth orbital flights of NASA's space shuttle, a "benchmark" for the reusable space transportation system that will significantly reduce costs and make access to space a matter of routine. The versatile space shuttle gives us an entirely new range of capability for pursuit of the vast potential that space offers.

The first manned orbital test of the space shuttle, planned for late 1979, sets the stage for six such developmental flights and creates a new era of expanded capability beginning with the first operational mission in 1980.

More than sixty years ago, Congress created NASA's predecessor "aviation technology" agency, the National Advisory Committee for Aeronautics (NACA), "to supervise and direct the scientific study of the problems of flight with a view to their practical solution." The aviation technology role of NASA remains largely unchanged from the congressional directive of 1915. The agency's job is to probe the frontiers of flight in the earth's near atmosphere and to develop advanced technology for civil and military aircraft, with particular emphasis on the solution of aeronautical problems. Specifically, the aviation role is to help manufacturers produce more efficient commercial aircraft thus helping the U.S. economy to gain through jetliner sales at home and overseas. Also, the efforts improve flight safety for all aircraft users, help cut aircraft operating costs, and ease the environmental impact of flight by reducing noise and pollution.

NASA's aviation plans involve looking well into the future to anticipate tomorrow's needs and develop the necessary technology. Researchers are investigating such areas as V/STOL (vertical/short takeoff and landing) transportation, an environmentally acceptable and economically efficient second generation SST (supersonic transport), cargo aircraft of immense capacity that will dwarf even today's jumbo jets, and the hypersonic transport of the twenty-first century.

The greater part of NASA's aviation research is seeking new aeronautical technology for aircraft already flying and for those that are being developed for the future. Principal focus is on energy efficiency and cutting aircraft fuel consumption. NASA has identified technologies that collectively could cut fuel use in half. This potential savings is of enormous national economic significance, for each cent of price increase for foreign oil means $1,000,000,000 a year paid to foreign interests and denied to the American economy.

Fuel-saving research is not a search for a single giant breakthrough, but rather it is an effort to advance know-how in several key areas that influence consumption. The technology being developed offers added value in passenger safety and comfort, noise reduction, and reduced engine-exhaust emissions.

Aircraft engines deteriorate with use and age just as auto engines do. Worn parts induce fuel waste. NASA's Lewis Research Center at Cleveland, Ohio, is trying to determine the major causes of component deterioration, for example, which worn parts waste the greatest amounts of fuel, and how to extend the period of maximum effectiveness of these parts. From this research, it is expected that improved components—expected to be available by 1980—will lead to a 5 percent decrease in engine fuel consumption, the equivalent of the energy required to operate New York City and Chicago for a hundred years.

Also, NASA is performing research that could lead to an advanced, fuel-saving engine that would operate at higher temperatures and pressures, which would mean greater fuel efficiency. Its many components would be lighter, reducing overall engine weight. It also would have a "regenerative" system to recycle heat for additional thrust. This advanced engine, which could be in service by 1990, will offer a 10 percent reduction in fuel use, enough energy savings to supply the needs of the entire United States for three years.

Also, plane propellers are being redesigned by NASA researchers. It was once thought that the propeller had reached its limit when aircraft speeds reached 400 miles (643.7 km) per hour. The factor limiting how fast a plane can travel is the speed of the propeller's tip, which travels faster than the parts of the propeller nearer the hub. However, a second look at the propeller indicates that tip speeds can be increased considerably. Tests show that a turbine-driven, eight-blade propeller with *swept tips* can achieve high efficiencies at the speeds and altitudes at which jetliners fly. Turboprop engines offer better fuel economy than jets, and the propeller's comeback would allow for fuel savings of 20 percent.

The Dryden Flight Research Center is flight-testing an aircraft that incorporates a new control system that contributes to fuel economy. Called the Digital Fly-by-Wire

System, it employs motion sensors, electrical wires, and on-board computers instead of the conventional weighty complex of rods and linkages that normally drive control surfaces. The fast-reacting, computer-controlled electronic system provides the exact amount of control response for more stable flight. To the passenger, this system means a smoother, safer ride in turbulent air. To the designer, it means reducing plane weight and further cutting fuel consumption.

Not one of these advanced concepts is a "maybe" type of thing. Supercritical wings, the fly-by-wire system, and composite materials are already in flight-test status. Some will enter airline service gradually, being incorporated into existing jetliners. Others, needing further research, will appear in the next generation of aircraft a decade or so later. The collective results of these various concepts will result in a commercial airliner of 1990 that will bear little resemblance to today's aircraft.

Also, the flight plans are giving increased attention to "general aviation," the term used to describe civilian aircraft that are not commercial airliners. These planes, which number about 140,000 in America and fly more than all airline transports combined, range from single-seat craft to multipassenger business jets. The effort seeks new technology to improve performance, safety, fuel consumption, and noise control.

Examples of safety research include full-scale crash tests aimed at providing better protection for general aviation pilots and passengers in the event of accidents which occur at a very high rate. The research includes work toward preventing stalls and spins, which account for about 35 percent of fatalities resulting from general-aviation accidents. Also being developed is a family of general-aviation wings for more efficient flight, lower fuel consumption, and reduced noise and emission levels. In addition, ways of improving spray accuracy of agricultural aircraft are being looked into.

An important development is the *supercritical* wing. The wing airfoil has a different shape: it is flattened on top and the trailing edge curves downward. These design features delay the buildup of air drag at high subsonic speeds, allowing the plane to fly faster or farther without increased fuel consumption. This is due to the improved aerodynamics, which reduces air resistance thus saving fuel because the engine does not have to work as hard. So future airliners will have wings that look more like those of sailplanes, allowing the plane to fly 15 percent farther with the same fuel load.

Another effort seeks to smooth the layer of air next to the aircraft's skin—the *boundary layer,* as it is called. Normally this air is turbulent, creating drag and wasting fuel. The *laminar flow* concept—laminar means smooth— calls for removing the turbulent air by suction, drawing it through porous aircraft surfaces by lightweight pumps. Smoothing the boundary layer affords fuel savings estimated at 20 to 40 percent.

Almost everyone knows that a lighter plane also eases the engine's work load. So, weight-trimming research focuses on new, lighter-weight composite materials such as graphite or boron woven into a matrix of resin or aluminum. These composites not only are lighter than the materials they would replace but they also are much stronger. They can reduce jetliner weight by as much as 25 percent and cut fuel consumption accordingly.

Also, in other avenues of research, NASA is probing a wide spectrum of aviation needs and problems. One plan involves cooperation with the Federal Aviation Administration in developing a system to prevent midair collisions, another with investigating the use of lasers to warn pilots of clear air turbulence ahead of the aircraft, and a third with redesigning landing gears to reduce *slush drag*—the retarding influence of runway snow and slush—which can keep a plane from reaching takeoff flying speed.

In these and a broad range of other related projects, NASA's space and aeronautical research are providing direct benefits in the form of technological spinoffs to airline passengers, operators, manufacturers, and shippers, as well as the general public.

TECHNOLOGY
TRANSFER TO MEET
SOCIETY'S NEEDS

Starting in 1975, some five million people in rural India watched daily television—which is extraordinary because India has no nationwide TV system.

An exciting and far-reaching demonstration known as SITE (Satellite Instruction Television Experiment) beamed TV shows to twenty-four hundred villages in India. SITE is the product of NASA's Applications Technology Satellite-6 (ATS-6). SITE uses direct broadcasting, sending its signals directly to simple, low-cost ground antennae by means of powerful on-board transmitting equipment. This unique capability eliminates the need for an elaborate and expensive ground complex of stations, antennae, amplifiers, and land lines. Direct broadcasting opens up a whole new world of opportunity to developing nations and regions, affording a means of providing education and entertainment in outlying areas where communications are either primitive or nonexistent. For the Indian experiment, SITE was put into orbit over Lake Victoria in East Africa, where the satellite could "see" all of India. From the cities of Delhi, Ahmedabad, and Amritsar, the Indian government transmitted specially prepared television programs to SITE, which rebroadcast them to the villages. Each village was provided with a 23-inch (58.4-cm) TV set for community viewing and an inexpensive aluminum dish antenna to pick up the signals.

SITE was an outstanding success, acclaimed by villagers and government officials alike. The community set was used for an hour and a half each morning as a teaching aid for children. In the evening, adults—many of whom had never heard of TV—turned out in large numbers for two-and-a-half-hour sessions divided equally between entertainment and practical instruction. A typical evening show included short features such as "Festivals and Fairs" and "Folk Music from Elsewhere," together with adult education discussions on nutrition, hygiene, and family planning. The top-rated shows, which had audiences begging for reruns, were those on pest control and how to increase crop yield.

When the year-long SITE experiment was concluded, NASA then conducted similar demonstrations in some thirty African countries over a three-month period, showing how satellite communications can quicken the pace of national development by improving commerce and education. Then, SITE was orbited back to the Western Hemisphere—over Ecuador—for a new series of experiments, including direct broadcasting to Latin America.

People in the United States, Canada, and Mexico might think that the communications problem does not apply in highly developed North America. But, it does—in places like Alaska, northern Canada, the Rocky Mountains, and Appalachia. In these and other areas, earth-based communications have not kept pace with the march of progress, and population density is not sufficient to justify the large, expensive ground complex needed to tie into the commercial communications satellite network. The utility of the direct-broadcast satellite in such remote areas was explored in an experiment called the Health/Education Telecommunications (HET) Experiment, jointly sponsored by NASA and the Department of Health, Education, and Welfare. In HET, the direct-broadcast satellite was used in an extensive study which checked out such potential applications as improving health care in remote areas and conducting educational seminars by means of satellite communications.

In a follow-up to that effort, NASA and the Canadian Department of Communications are working jointly on a project called Communications Technology Satellite (CTS). Launched in 1976, CTS has transmitting power levels ten to twenty times higher than current commercial communications satellites. Like SITE, the new satellite provides reception by low-cost antennae affordable by most communities. A number of public service experiments, such as satellite-supported medical treatment, classroom education, and high-speed data transfer for businesses are contemplated.

Another example of this kind of spinoff is the meteorological satellite. Most TV viewers are familiar with the National Operational Meterological Satellite System, in which NASA-developed satellites operated by the National Oceanic and Atmospheric Administration (NOAA) provide cloud-cover photographs and other information for interpretation by weather forecasters. The NOAA network has considerably enhanced routine weather prediction but perhaps the most striking benefit is in the detection and monitoring of severe storms—hurricanes and large frontal systems of a

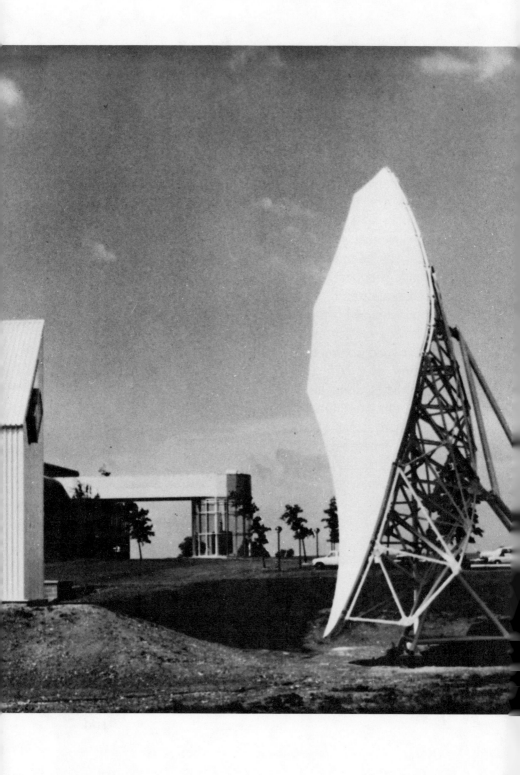

potentially destructive nature. The beneficial impact of meteorological satellites is demonstrated by the fact that since the inauguration of the operational satellite system in 1966, no major storm system has gone undetected at any point on the globe.

The public is not as well acquainted with some of the other uses of meteorological satellites. For example, the Geostationary Operational Environmental Satellites (GOES) are equipped with data collection systems for the acquisition and relay of environmental information from widely dispersed surface platforms, such as river and rain gauges, seismometers, tide gauges, buoys, ships, and automatic weather stations.

Weather satellite information is being used routinely to track the motions of the Gulf Stream for fishing interests and for the routing of coastal shipping. The U.S. Coast Guard uses cloud imagery to determine low cloud and fog conditions over the route of the International Ice Patrol, allowing cancellation or redirection of reconnaissance flights. Satellite infrared imagery provides the basis for drawing composite ice charts of the Great Lakes and Alaskan coastal waters. Estimates of the amount of snow cover and rainfall over both the Unites States and Canada are made possible by the satellite data.

An important future satellite project is Nimbus G. The Nimbus research satellite focuses on demonstrating advanced technology for detecting and monitoring air and water pollution from space. In 1979, for the first time, this satellite will provide global data on concentrations and distributions of many stratospheric gases and aerosols.

From NASA's Goddard Space Flight Center in Mary-

[17]

**This COMSAT Antenna
monitors information from
several satellites simultaneously.**

land, a most important applications program with sweeping possibilities for earth resources is Landsat. Earth-surveying satellites, the three Landsats now circle the globe and between them they have the potential to scan the entire earth, except for polar and cloud-obscured regions, every nine days. They provide information of earth conditions in digital form and in pictures that offer enormous practical benefit in managing the planet's "earth resources."

The Landsat view from space offers several advantages to scientists, engineers, planners, and others. Landsat makes it possible to look at large portions of the earth at one time—over 13,000 square miles (33,670 sq km) in a single picture—thereby revealing great features, such as geologic faults, that are impossible to see from near-earth. The repetitive coverage provided by the continuously orbiting satellites allows monitoring of dynamic earth processes, such as crop-growing conditions and changing land use over time. Landsat's ability to view the entire planet within a short period of time enables a whole new dimension of interregional comparisons of such activities as urban growth and land-use patterns.

Landsat images are created on earth from digital data obtained by the multispectral scanner, which employs a combination of radiation detectors, a mirror, and an earth-viewing telescope. As the telescope scans the earth, visible and near-infrared light waves reflected from earth strike the mirror. The mirror bounces the light waves into banks of detectors that separate the light into four spectral bands —red, green, and two near-infrared bands (infrared is not visible to the human eye). The light in each band is further separated into sixty-four levels of brightness and this information is converted into electronic signals. Landsat's transmitter sends the signals to earth receivers at 15 million "bits" per second, and a computerized signal-deciphering system at the Goddard Space Flight Center translates the flow of data into imagery on photographic film.

An outstanding example of Lansat's utility is the project known as LACIE, or Large Area Crop Inventory Experiment. An inventory of crops is important because it provides the basis for predicting yield and planning distribution. Most countries lack such data, but now their farmers can look forward to bigger and better crops, thanks to LACIE.

Various types of vegetation reflect light or emit radiation (like heat waves) in different bands of the spectrum and in different intensities. Landsat's sensitive detectors can often tell the difference, and can be programmed to "see" one particular kind of vegetation. In the initial test, LACIE inventoried wheat in the Great Plains of the United States. The experiment then was extended to cover agricultural regions of other areas of the world.

There are other agricultural benefits offered by Landsat. For example, diseased crops can be made to show up in shades different from those of healthy crops. Since early detection of blight allows prompt corrective measures to prevent the spread of disease, this Landsat capability presents a tremendous potential for more effective management of global food resources.

Also, the Landsat satellite has demonstrated potential for detecting earthquakes through the location of faults and their movements, for detecting water pollution, monitoring floods so their devastation can be lessened, assisting in exploration for new oil and mineral resources, recording surface-mined land, inventorying sources of fresh water over large areas, providing maps of uncharted regions, monitoring sea ice, surveying forests and assessing fire damage—the list goes on and on. The monetary benefits of Landsat's spinoffs will probably in time more than equal NASA's budgets.

NASA developed an oceanographic satellite called Seasat-A to complement Landsat. It was launched in 1978. Seasat's assignment will be continuous reporting of ocean dynamics—of such phenomena as wave height and direction, surface winds, ocean temperatures, current and tide patterns, and ice field locations. Monitoring of these conditions on our coasts and on a global scale offers important benefits in a number of areas—for instance, ship routing, ship design, storm and iceberg detection, coastal disaster warning, and the directing of fishing fleets to most productive waters.

In addition to satellite technology, NASA is involved in technological applications in ground systems, another source of spinoffs. An example of a major applications program is one called ACTS (Activated Carbon Wastewater Treatment System).

ACTS originated in space research at a NASA laboratory. An engineer, testing various materials in search of a lightweight rocket motor insulator, built a device for manufacturing carbon by *pyrolysis,* or high-temperature heating without oxygen. Looking for a substance from which to make carbon, he discovered that sewage solids offered an excellent raw material. He also found that the resulting activated carbon was a fine agent for treating sewage.

From these discoveries evolved the ACTS development, in which filtered solid sewage is burned to make activated carbon and the carbon in turn is used to filter sewage. The filtering process produces water as clean as that resulting from conventional methods, but offers a number of advantages in reduced costs.

Another NASA applications project promising future benefit involves the use of water hyacinths to remove pollutants. Long regarded in the tropics and subtropics as colossal nuisances because their rapid growth clogs rivers and streams, the water hyacinths are getting a new image as useful and beneficial plants as a result of the discovery that they thrive on sewage. The plants absorb and metabolize astonishing amounts of nutrients and pollutants and therefore offer a means of cleaning waste-water lagoons.

Water hyacinths are employed as a natural filtration and purification system in Bay Saint Louis, Mississippi, where a 40-acre (16-hectare) waste-water lagoon receives raw sewage from six thousand households. The plants flourished on a feast of sewage and soon produced dramatic results—a large part of the noxious lagoon became a clean, beautiful flower garden. As a result of this and other experiments, water hyacinths show real promise for purifying polluted waters. They also have a bonus potential as a source of fuel and fertilizer, and as a protein and mineral additive to cattle feed.

These are some examples of how satellite and ground-system innovations, representing much broader NASA applications, are producing significant benefits to society in the way of spinoffs.

SPACE TECHNOLOGY'S TRANSFER TO EVERYDAY LIFE

Technology spinoffs have applications for almost every facet of our lives. The steady stream of technology spinoffs has found its way into brain surgery and cancer treatment; home design and kitchen appliances; pollution control and waste disposal; fire prevention and protection of fire-fighters; law enforcement; airline safety; and transportation, energy systems, industrial processes, food products, bridge construction, farm machinery—the list can be extended almost endlessly.

But spinoffs are not often recognized as such, perhaps because today, far into the twentieth century, we accept technological advancement as a natural heritage of our modern life. We are rarely curious about the origin of a useful innovation or the identity of the inventor. The 100,000 people who wear a rechargeable pacemaker, or the millions who admire the lines of this year's cars or use a minicalculator, or the persons who buy a well-insulated parka, or install a homeguarding device, are usually unaware that aerospace technology played a role in the creation of all these products.

When a plane goes down in a remote area, or when a ship encounters trouble on the high seas, their crews trigger radio beacons which automatically send out distress signals. But there is little assurance that anyone will respond to the call for help, because there is still no adequate method of monitoring the signals and locating their source. As a result, thousands of lives annually are jeopardized in aircraft and ship emergencies.

Aerospace technology offers an answer to this critical problem—a spaceborne system of quick detection and location of distress signals. Called the Satellite Search and Rescue System, it is a boon to search and rescue operations that will vastly increase the probability of saving lives. This project originated almost two decades ago when NASA pioneered development of communications and weather satellites, improved versions of which are now operating routinely and providing practical benefits of great value.

Also, NASA is conducting some far-reaching tests of a nonatmospheric nature. One test employs ground-based laser radar to determine the spread of polluting particles exhausted from industrial smokestacks. Another involves the use of computerized "image enhancement" techniques, developed for planetary explorers like Viking and Voyager, to improve detail in undersea photographs.

The Viking Lander vehicles, while on the surface of Mars, presented one of the most interesting experiments ever conducted in space. This was an experiment in which the robot spacecraft scooped up soil samples, analyzed them automatically, and reported the findings back to earth. That soil-analysis system was one of the thousands of innovations of NASA's aerospace technology to be used in industry. The system can be converted to a practical instrument for use on earth. It has been used in a portable unit for measuring soil moisture prior to road construction to assure proper compaction of the roadbed. This technique is more rapid and less expensive than existing methods for testing surfaces because the analysis can be performed on-site.

Spinoffs do not just happen. They result from carefully planned, well-organized efforts. Congressional members, to assure American taxpayers a maximum return on their aerospace investment, directed NASA to spread as widely as possible the knowledge acquired in its research and to promote actively the secondary use of this wealth of technology. This congressional charter brought about the establishment, in 1962, of NASA's Technology Utilization division, which promotes spinoff planning at early stages of development and operations, actively seeks to improve industrial interests, publishes information about the availability of the many different potential transfers, and provides assistance to users.

There are a variety of ways in which spinoffs are brought to the marketplace. One of the most popular with business is the computer program package. NASA maintains one of the world's largest libraries of computer programs. It is called COSMIC (for Computer Software Management and Information Center). About sixteen hundred programs —or "software packages"—are available. COSMIC programs can perform tasks as diverse as determining a building's energy requirements, designing electronic circuits, optimizing mineral exploration, and drawing maps of water-covered areas using NASA satellite data. With an increasing number of business firms turning to Automated Data Processing (ADP) computer operations for greater efficiency, this facet of the spinoff process is paying big dividends to users. The results are reduced costs for companies because the software package can be used with most computers already available.

Among the many software packages is a structural analysis program called FEDGE. For example, the Babcock and Wilcox Company of Alliance, Ohio, used FEDGE in the design of a nuclear steam generator pressure vessel. FEDGE provided substantial savings by allowing computer modeling of the structure, as opposed to manual use of the mathematical data.

NASA further promotes technology transfer through seven Industrial Applications Centers, which offer one of the world's largest banks of technical data—more than eight million documents. This vast storehouse of technical knowledge can be a bonanza for businessmen exploring new markets, looking for answers to problems, or simply trying to stay competitive by keeping their technical people abreast of the latest developments in their fields. For a nominal fee, a client can get a computer search of the literature available in their particular area of interest and the help of NASA applications engineers in applying the results of the search.

One example of such a search is that of the Youngstown Sheet and Tube Company, which specializes in the manufacture of flat rolled steel, tubular and bar products. Since 1974, the company has had a continuing participation agreement with the NASA Industrial Applications Center at the University of Pittsburgh. The Center carried out more than thirty different searches for the company. One of the searches led to a company decision to change an industrial process; the change brought about savings of several hundred thousand dollars a year and a product improvement of sales of over a million dollars a year.

Also under the Technology Utilization Program, NASA assists in the solution of problems in such areas as safety, health, transportation, and environmental protection.

An example is the firefighter's traditional breathing apparatus which is heavy and cumbersome. It creates a problem described by a Boston deputy fire chief as follows: "Many firefighters prefer not to use the old equipment. They risk being overcome by smoke because if they use the old masks the weight can cause them to collapse from heat and exhaustion."

NASA's Johnson Space Center at Houston, Texas, developed as a countermeasure a long-duration, light-weight air bottle patterned on technology originally developed for rocket motor casings. The center also redesigned the breathing system's pack frame and harness. The resulting pack, produced by Scott Aviation of Lancaster, New York, weighs 40 percent less than existing equipment and is easier to handle because of its better weight distribution. In 1976, Boston became the first municipality in the nation to introduce the NASA-developed breathing apparatus as regular equipment and many more cities will soon follow suit.

In an associated effort, NASA's Marshall Space Flight Center, in Huntsville, Alabama, is working with the department of Commerce's National Fire Prevention and Control Administration in Project FIRES (Firefighters' Integrated

New firefighting equipment like this transportable unit have been developed by NASA technology.

Response and Equipment System). FIRES seeks to improve the firefighters' "envelopes," the various elements of protective clothing and equipment used in actual firefighting.

NASA sponsors applications teams, composed of experts in several different technological fields, to work with public-sector groups. There are three such biomedical and two technology teams located at various research institutes and universities. They tackle specific problems or accept challenges on the premise that aerospace knowledge might offer clues of solution where none are otherwise apparent. An example of this application is a case in which the biomedical team at the Research Triangle Institute, North Carolina, studied a problem sometimes experienced by those who suffer from arthritis or have suffered an injury, a stroke, or a bad burn. The problem is that when a hand is immobilized for a long period of time, it becomes progressively more rigid due to lack of exercise. Treatment requires a trained therapist to work the fingers for long periods daily, a painful process that is tedious to the patient and expensive.

The team devised a simple but valuable spinoff from airflow control technology. It was a pneumatically operated glove which fits over the hand and automatically flexes the fingers. The patient thus can conduct his or her own therapy. The glove frees the therapist for other duties, and there is a psychological bonus in the patient's knowledge that he or she can control the rate of finger movement and use the glove at any time to stop the pain. The finger flexor is now in regular use at many hospitals.

Product diversification by NASA contractors is another way in which aerospace technology is transferred to the commercial sector. An example is offered by the Hamilton Test Systems of Windsor Locks, Connecticut. Under NASA contract, they developed an environmental control and life-support system for a prototype space station. Included in this development was a system whose job was to monitor the performance of various pieces of equipment, detect failures, and identify a specific malfunctioning unit. The technology thus acquired provided a springboard to a commercial product called "Autosense," a computer-operated diagnostic system for isolating malfunctions in cars and trucks. Autosense, an automated "doctor," goes much further than some older diagnostic devices. In just twenty-five minutes, it can run through a "total auto health check," comparing operation of each part with factory specifications. The system is employed by used car, and even new-car dealers to satisfy customers that the vehicle they are buying is in tip-top shape. In use at repair stations, Autosense not only identifies trouble but also tells the mechanic —and the customer—why a faulty component is bad and how it may be fixed. After repairs have been made, a second health check printout shows the customer that the problem has been corrected.

An inventor working for an aerospace contractor helped customize a previously developed fire-retardant coating for use as part of the heat-shielding system for a manned spacecraft. He acquired patent rights to the material and formed a new company called Thermo-Systems. The company is producing a commercial line of fire retardant coatings which are meeting widening acceptance in construction of office buildings, manufacturing plants, schools, and a variety of other buildings, manufacturing plants, schools, and a variety of other buildings.

Sold under the trade name Thermo-Lag, the coatings work on the principle of *sublimation*. A subliming material —dry ice is the most familiar example—vaporizes, without melting, at a certain temperature, absorbing heat in the process. Thermo-Lag, which is sprayed or brushed onto building components like steel beams and electrical cables, contains compounds that sublime. When they sublime, they absorb heat from the flame as well as form a porous char layer which serves as highly efficient insulation. In this manner they retard the spread of flames and delay ignition of combustible materials. The company offers highly effective coatings for application to metal, wood, and even paperboard.

NASA especially encourages nonaerospace businesses to take advantage of the technological know-how. The more than ten thousand distinct innovations judged to have commercial potential have been identified and are available to any U.S. company that wants to use them. To publicize this availability, NASA publishes a quarterly journal called *Tech Briefs,* which highlights the technical nature and significance of each innovation. Businessmen, scientists, and engineers can receive *Tech Briefs* simply by writing to NASA. Hundreds of companies and thousands of individuals have made profitable use of information contained in the *Tech Briefs.*

A typical firm using this information is the WED (Walt Elias Disney) Enterprises division of Walt Disney Productions which conducts research and development for the entertainment operations of the company. A WED engineer read a *Tech Brief* that described a NASA report on fatigue life of roller bearings. Hoping to find an answer to a problem the company was experiencing with axle failures on the "Autopia" fun ride, he requested a technical support package from NASA. Based on the information received, WED redesigned and replaced bearings of all 350 axles with a more durable bearing material which ended their problem.

Still another way U.S. industrial firms can profit from aerospace technology is through use of some thirty-five hundred inventions patented by NASA. Interested firms can get nonexclusive, and sometimes exclusive, licenses for the commercial use of these inventions.

Transfer innovations like the foregoing spinoffs occur daily, and the list of potential users continues to grow as new aerospace programs inject new know-how into the technology bank. Spinoffs contribute to an improved way of life.

INNOVATIONS IN MEDICINE FROM SPACE TECHNOLOGY

Recent innovations such as providing good health care in space by "remote direction," an automated disease detector, a voice-controlled wheelchair, and a device that enables the blind to read almost anything in print are among a wealth of medical spinoffs being transferred from the world of aerospace to the public. In medicine, where lives are involved, there is no one best spinoff for they all count, but some past ones that are very important are the hand-held X-ray instrument, the portable echo-cardioscope and a "spinback" of a spinoff that will let us know if there is any form of life on Mars.

NASA is planning now toward the day of long-duration flight—perhaps even manned interplanetary missions —wherein routine health care and emergency treatment must be accomplished on board the spacecraft over periods of months or perhaps even years. Since spacecraft design limits crew size, the medical assignment may be handled by a single astronaut-physician or by a crew member trained as a physician's assistant. In a space emergency requiring surgery, for instance, sophisticated communications equipment, backed by a computerized data processing system, would make it possible for a surgeon on earth to "examine" the patient. The surgeon could study X rays and other data, specify an in-flight surgical procedure, and guide the astronaut-medic step by step through the operation.

Millions of people all over the world live in areas almost as remote as astronauts living in space. These people can benefit enormously from a system that enables a physician to help patients located great distances from his office or hospital.

Ka Ka, Hickiwan, Vaya Chin, and Gu Vo sound like places in China. They are not; they are American. They are villages of the Papago Indian Reservation in Arizona and they rank among some of America's most out-of-the-way places. As such, the villages have benefited from a significant transfer of space technology to health care for people in remote areas, where access to regular medical service is inadequate or nonexistent.

This spinoff is called STARPAHC (Space Technology Applied to Rural Papago Health Care). NASA technology in space communications and data processing is being applied to remote health services for the Papago tribe. It is a joint project involving NASA and the Indian Health Service of the Department of Health, Education, and Welfare, and the Papago's Executive Health Council.

The Papago Indian Reservation is truly remote, lying in the Sonora Desert, an arid, sparsely vegetated terrain, alternately flat and humped by clusters of mountains.

Sprinkled over some 4,300 square miles (11,137 sq km) are seventy-five villages where almost ten thousand people live. The principal Papago town of Sells is 70 miles (1,127 km) from Tucson. Many of the villages are more remote, even from Sells, but distance is only part of the travel problem. Although there are some paved highways, many roads are unpaved, slow, and very hazardous to travel after heavy rains.

A key element in servicing the remote areas of the reservation is the Mobile Health Unit, a large van containing clinical equipment and the communications gear for contact with STARPAHC's base of operations, the Indian Hospital at Sells.

Operating on a preannounced schedule, and staffed by a Community Health Medic (CHM) and a laboratory technician, the mobile clinic negotiates the rough roads of the reservation, visiting the villages in turn and handling as many as twenty-seven patients daily.

In the van's reception room, the medic interviews the patient to find out the complaint, symptoms, and other details. If necessary, the medic can call up the patient's medical history from records stored in Albuquerque by punching keys on a data terminal.

In the examining room, the medic conducts the examination under the supervision of a physician at Sells, who may watch on TV and converse on the radio link. If the physician wants to view a particular part of the body, the medic operates a color TV camera mounted overhead to transmit a close-up picture. When biochemical analysis

This mobile infant monitoring unit is used in emergency situations.

is indicated, the laboratory room can handle a variety of tests and send the results immediately to the doctor as data or even as microscopic slides transmitted by TV. The mobile clinic can also transmit X-ray pictures.

At the Sells hospital, "mission control," the supervising physician sits at a console containing TV monitors, together with a number of displays designed to provide necessary information. A major feature of the console is a control that enables the physician to direct the movement of the cameras in the mobile clinic many miles away. The physician can see, talk with, and, in a figurative sense, "touch" the patient. With the equipment and information available, the physician can make a timely diagnosis and specify treatment to be carried out by the medic in the mobile van.

The acceptance of STARPAHC by the various communities has been exceptional. Residents of the outlying villages depend on scheduled visits of the Mobile Health Unit and the daily services of the fixed clinic.

The system opens up a broad new potential for improving health care. The capability to communicate with remote villages suggests expanding TV instruction in areas such as environmental health, sanitation, nutrition, and disease control. STARPAHC's initial success makes it likely that its remote health-care activities will be continued.

Among a variety of diagnostic tools brought forth by space research are new methods of testing blood. As part of a plan to develop techniques for monitoring astronauts' health on long-duration flights, NASA contracted with Orion Research of Cambridge, Massachusetts, to produce a compact bloods analysis system. As a spinoff from this work, Orion manufactures a pair of typewriter-sized devices that simplify and speed blood analysis.

An important blood electrolyte, ionized calcium is necessary for blood coagulation, nerve function, and normal skeletal and cardiac muscle contraction. Earlier methods of measuring ionized calcium in blood were complex, requiring the use of highly skilled technicians. Orion's development is a simply operated, flatbed box that makes ionized calcium determination a routine clinical test. It is called Space Stat-20 (the "Stat" is from the Latin *statim,* meaning "immediate").

A very small blood sample is injected into the machine, where an electrode converts the ionized calcium concentration directly into an electrical signal. In less than three minutes, the value appears on a digital display. It speed of operation is important where rapid analysis is essential—during surgery, for instance.

Gemeni, a new chemical-testing instrument, which can determine a broad range of blood components is the latest of a NASA family of miniature centrifugal analyzers. It was developed originally for the Energy Research and Development Administration and for NASA's space shuttle. Gemeni can handle twenty blood samples simultaneously. It can make twelve tests of each sample to determine levels of blood sugar, calcium, cholesterol, albumin, glucose, uric acid, and other constituents. It can accomplish in thirty seconds tests that would take fifteen to twenty minutes by manual methods. The first working model was installed in a U.S. hospital in 1976.

Another important technology transfer is the "space imagining" technique discussed earlier, which can have important applications in diagnostic medicine: getting clear X-ray images of soft parts of the body is difficult because they are blocked by bone. One example of this involves early detection of lung cancer, which is vital but often difficult because, in the X-ray picture, the bone structure of the rib cage obstructs the view of the underlying lung tissue. To get a better picture of soft tissue, radiologists use internal dyes and radioactive substances, but

these methods do not always produce good results, and they can be uncomfortable for the patient.

A promising improvement in soft-tissue imaging utilizes filters such as those employed on NASA's Landsat earth-resources satellite. Landsat images can be filtered so that a specific area of interest shows up prominently and other areas are subdued. Landsat can be instructed, for instance, to survey a wheat crop, and the wheat will appear in a distinct tone.

The Goddard Space Flight Center is adapting these image-processing techniques to X-ray usage. The simple and inexpensive system consists of a filter and an optical decoder. The filter is placed between the patient and the X-ray apparatus. Using the lung-cancer example, the filter blocks out the bone and the optical equipment projects a clearer picture of the lung tissue.

It gets pretty hot on the moon. NASA, in solving the heat problem on the moon, has given another space technology innovation to the medical world. Because there is no atmosphere to impede the sun's rays, the temperature may rise as high as 250 degrees F (121 C). For that reason, astronauts working on the lunar surface wore a special suit consisting of a nylon outer layer supporting an inner network of tubing. Cool water flowing through the tubes kept the moonwalker comfortable. Researchers with NASA have made advances in the Apollo space suit design that offer highly efficient temperature control, and they have applied this technology to development of a water-cooled, brassiere-like garment being studied as an aid in the detection of breast cancer.

The Scanoprobe uses sound to "see" inside this animal.

Normal tissue gives off less heat than cancerous tissue and this forms the basis for a cancer-detection technique known as infrared thermography. However, it has been difficult to interpret thermograph results for detecting cancer in its earliest stages. The liquid-cooled garment being evaluated by the Breast Cancer Detection Demonstration Center in Oklahoma City cools the breast to improve reading of the thermograph image. Cancerous tissue recovers from cooling faster than normal tissue because of the increased blood flow characteristic of cancerous tumors. By increasing the temperature difference between normal and cancerous tissue through cooling, the differentiation becomes more apparent on the thermograph.

Since 1975, the Children's Hospital at Stanford assisted by NASA and the Stanford Biomedical Application Team, has been applying biotelemetry to the cerebral palsy problem. Children with cerebral palsy who suffer from muscular spasticity and loss of coordination will soon have another NASA space transfer to aid them. Many of these children who have great difficulty walking because certain muscles are in a constant state of contraction will have their problem eased. Surgical techniques can lengthen muscles or tendons to improve the child's walking pattern but it is vital for diagnosing accurately the particular spasticity problem of each patient. The individual muscles causing the handicap vary greatly from child to child. It is difficult by physical examination alone to determine precisely which muscle groups are most involved. Biotelemetry has provided a solution.

Biotelemetry, used extensively throughout space research to observe astronauts' vital functions from the ground, is the monitoring of body signals sent by radio wave. In the cerebral palsy application, the signal is the EMG—for electromyogram—which indicates the activity of the leg muscles. The advantage of biotelemetry is that it needs no wires. Other methods of monitoring EMG involve wires connecting a sensor on the patient to a recorder, thus interfering with the subject's normal walking pattern. It is very important to the children with cerebral palsy to have freedom of movement. They frequently have an impaired sense of balance and lack the muscle control necessary to protect themselves when they fall. Telemetry offers a means for unencumbered recording of the child's true gait pattern. This information is extremely helpful to the physical therapist and the orthopedic surgeon in determining the need for corrective surgery, evaluating various types of braces, and deciding whether certain muscle-relaxing drugs might prove effective.

NASA and Children's Hospital at Stanford, with the help of L and M Electronics Company of Daly City, California, introduced an improvement that eliminates the waist pack and the connecting cables previously used. Miniature transmitters, about the diameter of a large coin, are fastened directly over the muscle group being studied. They are painless. Each transmitter has its own tiny battery and a pair of sensing electrodes. Because they are small and lightweight, several transmitters can be used to broadcast EMG signals from both legs simultaneously.

The Children's Hospital at Stanford now has this important advance in active use for the cerebral palsy application. It appears to have broader potential because it could be used for monitoring other types of physiological signals where biotelemetry offers an advantage.

Another NASA space age innovation will soon benefit many people who have serious cataract problems. A cataract is a condition in which the lens of the eye becomes opaque (rather than transparent), restricting vision and leading to potential blindness. Surgery to remove the cloudy material is necessary to restore vision. More than 400,000 people a year need such surgery in the United States alone. The traditional surgical technique requires a 180-degree incision, and then numerous stitches to close it. Since the possibility of infection is high, patients are kept in the hospital up to ten days after surgery.

Cleveland eye surgeon Dr. William J. McGannon, the Retina Foundation of Boston, and NASA, in seeking to improve this technique have joined together to apply advanced technology in the fields of fluid mechanics, high-speed rotating machinery, miniature mechanisms, pumps, seals, and bearings. The resulting cataract surgery tool is a tiny cutter-pump which liquefies and pumps the cataract lens material from the eye. Inserted through a small incision in the cornea, the tool can be used on the hardest cataract lens. The cutter is driven by a turbine that operates at about 200,000 revolutions per minute.

Three years of effort have produced a design, now clinically being evaluated, with excellent potential for the improved cataract surgery. The use of this tool is expected to reduce the patient's hospital stay and recovery period significantly.

Duke Lumsden operates a candy shop in Tacoma, Washington. Duke is blind, yet he has no trouble differentiating between the values of currency he handles in the course of business because he is aided by a spinoff from space-developed optical-electronic scanning technology known as the Paper Money Identifier (PMI).

It's not distinguishable by the human eye, but each denomination of American currency has a unique distribution of patterns. This fact enables the PMI to tell the difference between different denominations of paper money.

The size of a cigarette pack, the device emits a narrow beam of invisible infrared light. This beam reacts to the reflectivity of the patterns on the bill and causes an oscillator to generate an audible signal. As Duke passes his PMI lengthwise along the back of a bill, he hears a distinctive series of tones that identifies each denomination.

Duke is very pleased with the paper money identifier, which he received from Tacoma's Technology Transfer Center. He not only handles paper money with ease, but he has discovered another use for the device. Before receiving the PMI, he had difficulty operating his tape recorder because he couldn't determine which track the tape was using; now his PMI tells him, by reacting to the different colors on the switch button light.

Another spinoff aid to the sightless is called the Optacon, by means of which a blind person may be reading this very printed page. The Optacon is an important advance for the blind and the deaf-blind, because it permits them to read almost anything in print, not just braille transcriptions.

NASA optical and electronic technology and research performed at the Stanford Research Institute developed the concept behind the Optacon. It gets its name from Optical-to-TActile CONverter. It works by converting regular ink-print into a readable, vibrating tactile form. The blind reader moves a miniature camera across a line of print with one hand while the index finger of the other hand is placed on the system's tactile array. As the camera moves over a letter, the image is simultaneously produced on a tactile array by small vibrating rods. The reading finger feels the enlarged letter as it passes over the tactile screen.

The standard training course covers fifty hours in nine days. The reading speed after training varies from student to student, the average being about ten words a minute. After considerable practice, speeds of forty words a minute are common and speeds as high as ninety words per minute have been achieved.

A whole new world for the blind is opened up by the

Optacon. They are no longer limited to material that has been tape-recorded or brailled. It enables them to carry out a great many everyday reading tasks.

The Optacon makes educational and instructional materials of the sighted available to the blind. It helps the sightless to obtain jobs, win promotions, and enter vocational areas previously closed to them.

In one application, a typewriter attachment permits a blind secretary to read what she is typing, to make corrections, and to fill out printed forms. Another accessory allows a blind engineer or scientist to read the visual display of an electronic calculator.

A portable echo-cardioscope has been adapted for people on earth from monitoring heart functions of astronauts. It replaces the need for inserting tubes in blood vessels (through which X-ray motion pictures are taken). The echo device forms images of internal organs using high-frequency sound—in somewhat the same way that underwater objects are detected from submarines using sonar.

Other ultrasonic imaging equipment also has been transferred from space use in an effort to substitute it for the harmful X rays. A new system is capable of resolving body-tissue images that are comparable with the quality of those from X rays. The first clinical trials were under way in 1978 with a goal of detecting breast cancers.

But until ultrasonics replace X rays for that purpose, still another space development is helping physicians reduce the quantity of X-ray exposures. Typically, doctors take more than one picture to expose an X-ray film properly. Now, solar cells that convert sunlight to electricity on space satellites can make a single exposure suffice.

Since solar cells are sensitive to X rays as well as light, a sensor made from such a cell is placed directly beneath the X-ray film and determines exactly when the film is exposed to optimum density. Not only was the X-ray hazard reduced significantly in a trial project at a Pasadena hospital, but the number of patient examinations was doubled. The sensors are especially useful in breast radiography. Since the breast is transparent to X rays, very low energy X rays must be used, requiring exacting exposures.

Space research has been transferred to cancer therapy, too. White blood cells and bone marrow—often destroyed along with cancerous cells in leukemia treatment—now can be stored for future use, just as blood plasma is kept in blood banks.

Previous attempts to freeze disease-fighting blood cells and bone marrow either destroyed the cells by rupture when cooled too fast or by dehydration when too slow. A special circuit developed for precise temperature control of scientific instruments aboard the Mars-bound Vikings has been adapted to a new freezing unit using liquid nitrogen. An evaluation unit, which can freeze white blood cells in an hour, was delivered in 1977 to the National Cancer Institute.

Also remember the suits the lunar astronauts wore between splashdown and their quarantine on the recovery ship? Designed to protect the environment from unknown microorganisms, similar suits now protect immune-deficient children and patients suffering from leukemia, burns, or other infections that can kill. The suits make it possible for such patients to leave their isolation rooms for up to several hours.

A whole new line of medical instruments that measure the ventilation of the lungs, which can help treat diseases such as emphysema, have been spun off from an analyzer that detects the composition of the atmosphere from satellites.

This year, a modification of the device allows a single

nurse to monitor up to fifteen patients by watching a television screen. A "spinback" of the instrument is helping to determine whether life is present on Mars.

The Viking mission has contributed to the mundane problem of decontaminating hospital oxygen systems in another development. The unlikely relationship proceeds as follows: technology developed to sterilize the Vikings utilizes a dry-heat technique ideal for sterilizing ventilators and other oxygen equipment.

The apparatus typically is contaminated from previous patient use. Chemical disinfectants remove most of the microorganisms. But the few that are left multiply rapidly in the humid oxygen. A NASA laboratory helped redesign one manufacturer's equipment using space-type plastics and new methods of sealing compartments.

A concept fostered by a NASA scientist for studying X-ray sources in space has led to a hand-held X-ray instrument that produces an instant image with a small source of radioactive material.

Powered by a single pen-sized battery, the prototype model of the rugged device exhibits high potential for screening and other uses in medicine, dentistry, and areas of industry. The most obvious promise of the unique unit is for emergency and other field use where a quick fluoroscopic examination is desirable, such as examining premature babies that can't be moved or evaluating injuries in remote areas where heavyweight and costly X-ray equipment is not available.

The new device is called a Lixiscope (Low Intensity X-ray Imaging Scope). It is based on the concept of researching energy sources in space by converting their X rays to visible images. The device was developed by Dr. Lo I. Yin, an X-ray researcher at the Goddard Space Flight Center.

Potential applications of the Lixiscope range from

examination of a football player's possible bone injury on the field to detection of welding defects or gas leaks in pipes.

The Optacon, the Lixiscope, and the other spinoffs mentioned in this chapter are but a sampling of the many examples of how space technology transfer is improving the status of millions of people, not only in the medical field, but also in the other fields of science and industry.

SPACE TECHNOLOGY AND THE ENVIRONMENT

A unique device for surveying forest lands highlights a number of spinoff developments benefiting environmental protection and resources management. The U.S. Forest Service has 187 million acres (75.7 million hectares) of land in forty-four states and Puerto Rico. Accurately marking the boundaries of such extensive property is obviously a monumental task. The Forest Service once estimated that, with conventional surveying techniques, it would take twenty-four years and cost $100 million to perform the job, but a NASA-developed system enables the Forest Service to do it in ten years and at considerable savings.

New emphasis on border marking of national forests has become necessary in recent years because of increasing use of adjoining land by private owners whose enterprises range from basic timber cutting to resort developments. A large percentage of forest land is not well enough marked to allow landowners to manage their properties with the confidence that they are not trespassing on government property.

The survey of land was originally estimated as a twenty-four-year job because the rough terrain—mountains, trees, and thick bushes—often blocks direct sighting between two points, the conventional method of surveying. To hack the sighting paths through the forests by axe and bulldozer is a costly and time-consuming process.

The Forest Service officials consulted NASA and found a solution in the application of laser technology originally developed for satellites. NASA-Goddard built a system called a "laser range pole," a portable, battery-operated, backpack device that allows direct sightings no matter how rough the intervening terrain or how thick the forest.

The equipment consists of a laser transmitter and a receiver. From a given property marker, the transmitter pulses a laser beam vertically, several thousand feet in some cases. At a second surveying point about a mile away, the receiver detects the laser pulse high above the trees, and locks in on the exact direction. Thus provided a bearing between the two points, a ground crew can extend the borderline back to the sending point by conventional surveying techniques.

The Forest Service now has several such lasers in use. The Department of the Interior's Bureau of Land Management also uses them for surveying vast land areas such as those in Alaska.

The environmental control of automobile emissions, another spinoff, is enhanced by new electronic systems devised during the Apollo space research. Many interesting technology transfers involve not merely a specific product, but rather a whole facility, its equipment, and the experience of the people who operate it. Chrysler Corporation's Huntsville, Alabama, facility provides a good example. Once a key test and development area for space research, the electronics division there is now primarily engaged in similar but non-NASA work. Its NASA work gave Chrysler a broad capability in computerized testing to assure quality control in development of solid-state electronic systems.

Today that division manufactures products not destined for NASA, most of them being associated with the company's automotive line. A major project is production and quality-control testing of the "lean-burn" engine, one that has a built-in computer to control emission timing, allowing the engine to run on a leaner mixture of fuel and air.

Other environment-related products include vehicle emission analyzers. The newest of the line is an accurate, portable, solid-state instrument for testing auto exhaust gases. The exhaust analyzers, now being produced for company dealers and for service stations, are expected to find wide use in state and municipal auto inspection.

Similar technology is employed in production of other exhaust analyzers, including systems to check out new engines in laboratory tests and units for testing new-car emissions to assure that they meet Environmental Protection Agency standards. The Automated System for Emission Testing (ASET) can coordinate as many as seven vehicle exhaust analyzers at one time. The Automotive Pre-Check Corporation of Los Angeles uses ASET to test about three thousand new cars each year, to comply with California air pollution laws which require that a 2 percent sample of all new cars sold in the state be exhaust-analyzed.

The General Electric Company as the NASA contractor on biosatellite research several years ago gained valuable experience in waste management and associated spacecraft environmental technology. The company has spun off this experience into packaged waste treatment systems for both sea and land use.

Their initial effort was a "shipboard waste treatment system," which used physical and chemical processes to clear waste-water, settle the solid matter, and remove harmful microorganisms. The solid residue is reduced to a small amount of ash by the system. They built and installed these sludge incinerator systems on an Army dredge, a Navy destroyer escort, and three Great Lakes steel-ore carriers.

Using the same technology, General Electric then built and tested a trial land-based system. This experiment evolved into an advanced 50,000-gallon-a-day (189,000 l) "packaged waste treatment system," installed in Jacksonville, Florida, by Demetree Builders of that city. The system now serves about six hundred units there in the Villa del Rio and Ortega Arms apartment complexes.

In another spinoff, the Alaskan oil flowing through the 800-mile (1,290-km) pipeline to the ice-free port of Valdez on the Gulf of Alaska is kept flowing thanks to an accomplishment of aerospace technology.

The fact is that the pipeline would never have been approved by Congress had it not been for the unique heat pipe, which is regularly used in spacecraft to cool electronic equipment. In the Alaska pipeline, heat pipes protect the tundra from thawing and causing pipe ruptures that could spill large amounts of oil over the land.

The heat pipe's job is to keep the arctic ground frozen. The permafrost soil alternately freezes and thaws with seasonal temperature changes, causing surface dislocations and problems for the builders. In winter, a phenomenon called frost-heaving uplifts the soil. It is something like the creation of highway potholes by the freezing of rainwater below the roadbed—but frost-heaving exerts far greater force. It is therefore necessary to keep the soil in a continually frozen state, to stop the powerful forces of frost-heaving which could weaken supporting structures and rupture the pipeline.

To do so, McDonnell Douglas Corporation applied heat pipe principles in the design of the vertical supports that hold up the 4-foot-diameter (1.22 m) oil pipeline in permafrost areas. There are some 76,000 McDonnell Douglas heat pipes varying in size—according to terrain requirements—from 2 to 3 inches (5 to 7.6 cm) in diameter and from 31 to 66 feet (9 to 20 m) long.

These space age technology transfers from NASA to the environmental resources field are but a few of many innovations available to make society's struggle an easier one.

ENERGY SAVINGS
FROM SPACE

NASA is applying its scientific and technical expertise in America's quest for new ways of producing and conserving energy. Of all the potential benefits of space, none perhaps is more exciting to an energy conscious world than an orbiting power station. The Satellite Power System is the most dramatic projected advance in a relatively new area of NASA effort: development of technology to meet future earth energy needs and to alleviate dependence on fossil fuel power. NASA's orbiting power station would be a large structure, perhaps several miles long, called the Satellite Power System. It would draw energy directly from the sun and beam it to earth receivers, producing enough electricity to meet the needs of a large city. The energy supply would be inexhaustible and virtually free of the pollution caused by today's fuel-burning electrical power generators.

[53]

The concept has already progressed beyond the dream stage. It was first proposed over ten years ago and has been the object of very intensive study in recent years. Although the technology needed is of enormous dimension, experts at NASA and the Department of Energy feel that the initial space-based power station could be operating in less than twenty years. One estimate holds that, by the year 2030, there could be 100 or more such satellites in orbit, generating a significant portion of the nation's energy requirement.

NASA has special capabilities for energy work. Since the start of the space age, the agency has been engaged in development of energy systems for spacecraft—solar cell arrays, for example, which supply electrical power for unmanned satellites, and fuel cell power-plants for the greater electrical demands of manned spacecraft. Examples of NASA's varied energy plans include development and demonstration of reliable, commercially acceptable solar heating and cooling equipment, advanced technology for methods of converting sun heat and wind energy to electricity, ways of increasing production in coal mining operations, measures to reduce the energy demands of industrial turbines, and new types of auto engines that could contribute significantly to fuel consumption.

The best example of the spinoffs in the energy field is "the house that NASA built" which is a space age demonstration of how advanced technology can cut home fuel consumption by up to two-thirds and water use by up to half while also providing bonuses in safety and comfort.

Homeowners would like to be relatively independent of rising utility costs and draw instead on nature's bounty for a significant part of their energy needs. Or, to put it another way, how would you like your house to have a special design and other features that could save your family over $20,000 in utility costs over a twenty-year period and at the same time offer a variety of innovations that add up to greater comfort, convenience, security, and fire safety?

Such a house already exists. Its development has been completed and its equipment and design features are available to the public. Most of the systems evolved from some aspect of space research. Each was selected to fit one of the guideline categories: money savings, safety, or comfort.

The home is called The Energy Conservation House (Tech) and was built at NASA's Langley Research Center in Virginia. Tech House incorporates NASA technology, the latest commercial building techniques and other innovations, all integrated into a superefficient home that offers exceptional savings to the individual family and potentially great national benefit in resource conservation.

In August 1977, a family moved into the home for a year's test while NASA engineers monitored the new systems and put together a record of day-to-day performance. The Tech House concepts influence long-term developments in home construction by pointing up the many benefits space age technology offers.

Tech House is a contemporary, one-story, three-bedroom home which could be available commercially in less than five years for about $50,000 (in today's dollars) excluding the lot—a price once in the luxury class but now in the American middle income level. It has a large living room with a fireplace, dining area, kitchen, three bedrooms, two baths, laundry, and garage. Tech House is not a prototype of a mass-producable design suitable for all locations. Rather, it is a research and development laboratory for testing innovations that can be applied to some degree in all housing.

The principal energy-saving comes from using the sun's rays to heat the home and to provide domestic hot water. Sunlight is captured by eighteen solar collectors on the roof. These south-facing collectors are angled at

58 degrees for best exposure to the Virginia winter sun. (In other latitudes, they would be mounted at different angles; 21 degrees plus the latitudes is optimum.) The individual solar collector has a glass outer plate and a metal inner plate, the latter coated with black chrome. The coating, developed in research on solar cells for spacecraft, prevents much of the heat from "reradiating," or escaping outward. Black chrome offers a 20 percent efficiency increase in the solar-collection process.

Running through the solar collectors are pipes through which water is circulated from a 2,000-gallon (7,500 l) underground storage tank. The water is heated by the sun's rays to a temperature of 140 to 170 degrees F (60 to 77 degrees C). When the house needs heating, the hot water passes through a heat exchanger, which extracts the heat and blows it through ducts to warm the home. When heating is not required, the water bypasses the heat exchanger and goes directly to the tank for later use.

For cooling the house, the heat pump system operates in similar fashion, except that it uses cool water; the cooler the water, the more efficient the pump. Water cooling is accomplished by radiators on the roof. At night, water from the storage tank is run through the radiators, heat is radiated out, and cooled water delivered back to the tank.

For domestic hot water, Tech House employs a two-stage "preheating" method. Water in one tank is heated by solar energy, then fed into another tank where an electrical system provides additional heating if required to reach a preset temperature level. Preheating by solar energy generally takes care of 80 percent of the hot-water energy requirement.

Tech House boasts a variety of other novel design features and systems to reduce energy usage.

The Tech House comfort control system allows substantial energy savings over a period of time. The computer-directed system heats or cools only the rooms actually in use at any given time and maintains precise temperatures. To accomplish this feat of heating intelligence, a computer is programmed based on the pattern of the occupying family's activities. If family habits change, the computer can be reprogrammed.

In case of a power failure, Tech House is lighted by an emergency electrical system developed by NASA for lighting the Skylab manned space laboratory. Individual "Satellight" modules use electronic fluorescent lamps that emit a great deal of area lighting with extremely low energy demand. Now widely used in industrial applications, Satellights feature exceptionally long life and are inexpensive to install. Three of them, strategically located, can light Tech House in an emergency. Satellight modules are powered by a 12-volt battery which is charged by a single solar cell, mounted on the roof of the garage.

Tech House enjoys its greatest energy savings in heating because it uses solar energy for a major part of the need. The supplemental heat pump does consume electricity when its use is required, but the electrical demand is reduced by the superefficient insulation. The gains are impressive with regard to central heating; in terms of annual kilowatt hours of energy, Tech House uses only a fifth as much as a contemporary comparison home.

Solar preheating of domestic hot water affords a similar advantage; the energy requirement for Tech House is roughly a third that of a comparison house. In eleven other categories of measurement—air conditioning, lights, refrigerator, oven, and so on—Tech House is designed to consume 12 to 60 percent less energy than a conventional

PRIVATE RESIDENCE

HOUSE CLOSED FOR ONE YEAR.
FAMILY LIVE-IN TEST.
WILL RE-OPEN IN SEPT. 1978
FOR PUBLIC INSPECTION....
....Available in Visitor Center...

house. A family of four in a typical house uses about 46,000 kilowatt hours of energy a year; in Tech House the same family would use only 15,000.

Energy usage is a big factor in economy and conservation, but water-use efficiency is also important to the homeowner. Water bills, like energy costs, are climbing and they can be expected to go higher (as mentioned earlier), at about the 10 percent annual rate predicted for energy. Individual considerations aside, water conservation is essential to the national interest in view of growing concern about possibly severe water shortages in the future.

A potential solution to the water conservation problem is the total recycling system in which waste water is recaptured, purified, and used over and over. However, such systems are not economically feasible and there is little chance that they will become cost-effective within five years, a basic guideline for selecting Tech House innovations. So designers compromised and built into the home a partial water reclamation system based on prior work at Langley Research Center on spacecraft systems for fluid recycling. Most waste water in Tech House is reused for toilet flushing, which accounts for almost 40 percent of a typical American family's water consumption. Tech House's family of four will use about 36,000 gallons (136,000 l) annually, well under half the equivalent usage of conventional house occupants.

While the basic thrust is toward utility economies, Tech House also serves as a proving ground for devices designed to provide greater home protection, many of them aerospace spinoffs. Fire safety begins with the home's insulation, all of it fireproof. Tripolymer, for instance,

Tech House uses energy-saving technology, like the solar panels on the roof.

simply forms a charred crust when exposed to flame or intense heat and it immediately extinguishes the flame.

The Tech House design takes due note that people are more security-conscious than ever these days. It offers an advanced security system that makes the home virtually intrusion-proof. The thermal shutters are part of it. When rolled down, they lock automatically and cannot be raised from the outside.

All of that—and more—is Tech House, a fascinating collection of energy innovations that offer exciting conservation prospects for the nation's future. Energy savings innovations are among the most important spinoffs offered to the public by NASA, with the prospect of its satellite power stations being the power savior of this country and the world when conventional energy runs out in a few decades.

SAFETY SPINOFFS

Over the years, while advances have been made in putting out fires, little has been done to predict them. "Knowing where a forest fire may occur and how it might act is almost as important as having the men and equipment to fight it," says William Innes, Jr., senior meteorologist for the California Division of Forestry (CDF). Few disasters are more devastating or more saddening than a raging forest fire. Even when no loss of life or property occurs, fire destroys an extremely valuable resource—the great trees of the forests.

Now a capability exists that may fill a long-standing need—an automatic system that sends fire-prediction information from remote forest sites to central offices by satellite. Made up of sensors originally developed for space applications, and a combination of solar energy, wind energy, and commercial power, the ground element of the system is a tiny weather station that can be set up in hard-to-reach locations and left to operate automatically for a year or more without maintenance. The first working units were set up in 1976. In mid-1977 the CDF had the initial complement of twenty-five working. Called automatic fire index stations, they were developed by NASA's Ames Research Center in cooperation with the CDF, a division of California's Department of Conservation.

As surprising as it sounds, for years, CDF's fire-prediction information came from daily fire-weather observations. Obviously, something more was needed. Innes explains: "More weather support is imperative. We need up-to-the-minute weather conditions to know when and where to send our attack forces to stop fires. Too many significant facts fall through the mesh when weather is sampled only once or twice a day."

Now, with the NASA system, the CDF gets fire-weather data from the Geostationary Operational Environmental Satellite (GOES) every three hours at headquarters in Sacramento. Three hours gives the firefighters enough lead time to control any fire in their area.

NASA-Ames built two prototypes and tested them within CDF forest areas before developing the final version —a relatively low cost system that weighs only 200 pounds (90.7 kg), can be transported to the most remote forest areas by three people, and can be set up in one hour.

Each monitor has a weather sensor, a transmitter, and a power supply. The weather sensor obtains information on wind velocity and direction, solar radiation, relative humidity, and the moisture content of inflammable forest litter—pine needles, leaves, and grass, for example.

The transmitter can send sensor data to the satellite —operating at an altitude of more than 22,000 miles (35,420 km)—using only 50 watts of power for short-burst transmissions. The transmitter is sealed in a waterproof can and buried within a 2-inch-thick (5 cm) redwood container.

The station's power is provided by a rechargeable storage battery. In the operational test system, three different types of energy sources for recharging are being explored: solar panels, a windmill, and commercial gasoline-powered (petrol-powered) generators.

The flow of weather data follows an elaborate path from the forest to CDF's Fire Protection Office. Because mountains and trees block direct line-of-sight transmissions, the weather information is routed first to the GOES satellite. GOES then retransmits the signals to a computer complex in the Washington, D.C., area where reports from each transmitting station are identified by a code number. The CDF data are then relayed by telephone tie-in to Sacramento, where another computer translates the information into a form usable for prediction. The entire process takes about an hour. This is a most important hour for it will greatly reduce the acreage of forests lost to fire, and homes and possessions in adjacent communities which would have been burned out. As the system proves itself, CDF envisions its spread to a statewide network providing data for the most effective use of firefighting resources.

In another benefit to society, a NASA spinoff helps trace criminals. A videotape storage and retrieval system originally developed for NASA has been adapted as a tool for law enforcement agencies.

Ampex Corporation of Redwood City, California, built a unique system for NASA. The first application of professional broadcast technology to computerized recordkeeping, it incorporates new equipment for transporting tapes within the system. After completing the NASA system, Ampex continued development, primarily to improve image resolution.

The resulting advanced system, known as the Ampex Videofile, offers advantage over microfilm in its filing, storing, retrieving, and distributing in digital code rather than in picture form.

Videofile is being used by a growing number of law enforcement groups in the United States and Canada, but its utility is not limited to police work. American Republic Insurance Company uses it for claims and rate analysis and it is in service with the Southern Pacific Railroad for filing half a million freight waybills monthly.

Another transfer is an improved air safety underwater locator device. Called the "Pinger," it uses sonar techniques to locate aircraft that have crash-landed in water— or, more specifically, to recover the flight recorder aboard the aircraft. The flight recorder provides clues as to what caused the accident and suggests measures to prevent similar future occurrences. Until recently, there was no way to recover flight recorders aboard planes lost in water crashes.

The Pinger, now serving 95 percent of the airline industry, provides a remedy. The key element of the Pinger system is a small, battery-powered transmitter, or homing beacon, included as part of the recorder package. For as long as thirty days, the transmitter sends out an acoustic signal from water depths up to 20,000 feet (6,096 m).

NASA's spinoffs also enter into the classroom. Trouble in schools is an unpleasant fact of modern life. Space technology can't stop the trouble from occurring but it can prevent it from spreading.

In recognition of this, NASA and the Sacramento, California, Unified School District developed a personal security system based on space telemetry technology. The first application was for schools, but the simplicity and reliability of the system have made it more widely applicable.

The heart of the system is an ultrasonic pen-sized transmitter. It can be used by prison guards, teachers, or by others such as the handicapped and the elderly.

When a problem arises, be it a threat of violence or a medical crisis, the pen transmits a silent signal to a nearby receiver. Within an institution, apartment, or office building, the receiver may be one of many that are wired to a central console that will display the exact location of the emergency.

Skidding causes many traffic accidents. Streets and highways with skid-resisting surfaces reduce the incidence of such accidents, help save lives, and reduce the high cost of replacing or repairing the damaged property. In fact, resurfacing roads to improve skid resistance is now required by federal law. Skid resistance is measured by road testing with specially equipped "skid" trailers. A special NASA-Langley project will considerably reduce the cost of "skid" trailers, thus making them more widely available to highway departments.

For testing the skid resistance of aircraft runways, Langley engineers developed a relatively inexpensive test vehicle and a "pulsed braking" technique that has been applied to road testing. Results exceeded expectations.

Another industrial spinoff originally developed for NASA's Apollo and Skylab manned spacecraft resulted in the creation of a whole new company to produce and market a special lighting system.

The "special lighting" system is a "Multi-Mode" electronic lighting system which is designed for plant emergency and supplemental use, such as high lighting, "always-on" stairwell lights, and illuminated exit signs. Their advantages stem from the higher quality demanded for spacecraft installation: extremely high light output with very low energy drain, compactness, light weight, and high reliability.

The firefighting aids, the improved method of tracing criminals, skid-proof technology, and the novel school-security device are but a few of hundreds of NASA's technology transfers that are helping to improve public safety.

[65]

FOOD
TECHNOLOGY SPINOFFS

Innovative ideas that are spinoffs from space technology offer better hospital food service, new equipment for food processing, and improved nutrition for the elderly.

If you have ever been in a hospital, you are probably aware of a problem that has long troubled the staffs of most large medical institutions. "Tired food," it is called. Food gets "tired"—even stale—when there is too long a lapse between preparation and delivery to the patient. This happens often in hospitals that must serve a thousand or more meals daily, because food must be cooked well in advance, stored hot until mealtime, then moved to nursing units some distance from a central kitchen. During this lengthy process, the meal loses heat and moisture, looks unappetizing and, most important, its nutritional value is diminished.

Food no longer need suffer this sort of fatigue, thanks to a space spinoff called the "integral heating system." The system features an entirely new concept of electronic food warming—no gas flame, no electric rods, no thermostats, no radiation. Now in use in numerous U.S. hospitals and nursing homes, it provides a means of serving warm meals with better appearance and taste retention, no burning or drying out, and no loss of nutrition.

The history of integrated heating can be traced back many years to a similar but less sophisticated 3M Company design intended for airline use, which was redeveloped as a food-service unit for manned spacecraft. The device uses less electricity because the heat goes directly to the food; it is not wasted by heating oven walls and surrounding air. Efficiency of the integral heating system is 90 percent or more—as compared to a range of 30 to 50 percent in conventional equipment.

Space telemetry has been transferred to food processing in the Armour Tenderometer, an instrument that predicts the tenderness of meat. The space component of the instrument is a sensitive, highly reliable strain gauge originally produced for NASA's Surveyor lunar lander and other space projects.

The Saturn V booster burns ultracold liquefied hydrogen fuel, which must be protected from the intense heat of the launch vehicle's mighty rocket engines. This necessitated development of superefficient insulation to keep the fuel tanks cold. One of two methods used was a spray-on polyurethane foam technique. The technique now has found commercial application as insulation for tuna boats.

Freshly caught tuna are stored below decks in wells cooled to about zero degrees by being circulated through a refrigerating system. The wells formerly were insulated

by cork or fiberglass but both materials were subject to deterioration; cork, for instance, needs replacement every three years.

People in the fishing industry say that foam insulation is far more reliable, efficient, and economical than previous techniques. More than forty foam-insulated tuna boats, ranging in cost from $1,000,000 to $4,000,000, have been built and sold.

Another spinoff to the food-processing industry involves a dry lubricant used in such spacecraft as Apollo, Skylab, and Viking. The lubricant is a coating bonded to metal surfaces providing permanent lubrication and corrosion resistance. The coating lengthens equipment life and permits machinery to be operated at greater speed, thus increasing productivity and reducing costs. Bonded lubricants are used in scores of commercial applications. They have proved particularly valuable to food-processing firms because, while increasing production efficiency, they also help meet the stringent USDA sanitation codes for food-handling equipment. For example, a cookie manufacturer plagued by production interruptions because sticky batter was clogging the cookie shapes, had the brass patterns coated to solve the problem. Similarly, a pasta producer faced USDA action on a sanitation code violation because dough was clinging to an automatic ravioli-forming machine. Using the antistick coating on the steel forming-plates solved their problems of sanitation deficiency and production line downtime and the transfer took its place among the many food technology spinoffs.

**Food processing and packaging
developed for the Apollo astronauts
is being produced for everyday use.**

SPINOFFS FOR INDUSTRIAL PRODUCTIVITY AND TRANSPORTATION

A versatile computer program for better design of structures is an important aerospace spinoff that is beneficial to industrial productivity and transportation.

A roller coaster isn't ordinarily associated with space technology. Except, of course, "Space Mountain," the exciting roller coaster ride at Disney World in Orlando, Florida.

The roller coaster was designed by Walt Disney Productions. The task was to design a support structure for the tracks that would be totally safe and yet not overly strong. Overstrengthening adds nothing to safety. It simply wastes money in unneeded steel. Disney engineers heard of a NASA-developed computer program that simplifies the job of analyzing structures and used it to gain substantial savings in work and materials. Success in the initial effort led to reuse in designing a similar ride at Disneyland in Buena Vista, California.

The roller coaster example is one of hundreds of cases where industry has benefited from NASTRAN, an acronym for NASA Structural Analysis Program. Since 1970, this has been available from NASA's Computer Software Management and Information Center (COSMIC) at the University of Georgia. Cost to the client averages $3,000 to $4,000 which is usually a mere token compared to the savings. In some cases, the NASTRAN investment has returned several millions of dollars. In most instances, the gain is more modest though still significant. Because NASTRAN is widely employed, it represents an enormous national economic benefit. One economic study estimated that in the period from 1971 to 1984, NASTRAN spinoffs alone will return more than $700 million to the U.S. economy.

NASTRAN is an offshoot of the computer-design technique used in construction of airplanes and spacecraft. In this technique, engineers create a mathematic model of the aeronautical or space vehicle and "fly" it on the ground by means of computer simulation.

From this base of aerospace experience, NASA-Goddard developed the general-purpose NASTRAN which offers an exceptionally wide range of analytic capability with regard to structures. NASTRAN has been applied to cars, trucks, rail cars, ships, nuclear power reactors, steam turbines, bridges, and office buildings.

NASTRAN is essentially a genuine crystal ball which takes an electronic look at a computerized design and reports how the structure will react under a great many different conditions. It can, for example, note areas where high stress levels will occur—potential failure points that need strengthening. Conversely, it can identify overdesigned areas where weight and material might be saved safely. NASTRAN can tell how pipes stand up under strong fluid flow, how metals are affected by high temperatures, how a building will fare in an earthquake or how powerful winds will cause a bridge to oscillate.

NASTRAN analysis is quick and inexpensive. It minimizes trial and error in the design process and makes possible better, safer, lighter structures while affording large-scale savings in research and development time and materials.

In another industrial spinoff, the O. Z. Gedney Company of Terryville, Connecticut, found the answer to a problem in a NASA Tech Brief describing research in adhesive bonding for the Space Shuttle. Gedney, which makes electrical fittings for industrial plants, was developing a new "fire stop," a device that prevents the spread of fire through holes where cables and pipes penetrate fire barriers in buildings.

NASA research is supporting the electric-car revival and making bridges safer, among many other advances in transportation. The electric car is staging a comeback. It burns no gasoline (petrol), a major advantage both to individuals and to the national aim of reducing petroleum imports. It is clean and quiet, offering a potential environmental boon.

In the United States and several other nations, researchers are taking a new look at the electric car. They are predicting that current shortcomings can be remedied and that an efficient battery-powered auto can be available in ten years. And space technology is playing a part in reviving a once-promising vehicle.

If you were born after World War II, chances are you don't remember the electric car. Invented in 1887, it provided strong competition for the gasoline-powered car in the first decade of this century. The "petrocar," as some called the gasoline-driven vehicle, was a noisy, smelly smoke-belcher. The noiseless electric car didn't frighten the horses that were everywhere in those days. And it was advertised as safer. Its battery needed recharging every 20 miles (32.2 km) or so, but that was not too great a disadvantage since nearly all car travel at the time was local.

After 1910, however, internal-combustion technology advanced rapidly while electric-auto technology stagnated. The electric car still held the noise advantage but its lack of range caused its downfall as a network of roads and highways burgeoned and car touring became the rage. Electric vehicles then faded gradually from use.

The battery is the key to the electric car's possible comeback as a passenger vehicle. Studies show that a car capable of averaging 82 miles (132 km) a day on a single battery charge would meet 95 percent of the need for a full-service city vehicle. Present commercially available batteries which have lead electrode plates in an acid solution can't meet the 82-mile-a-day requirement.

NASA's Lewis Research Center in Cleveland, Ohio, undertook research toward a practical, economical battery with higher energy density. Borrowing from space satellite battery technology, Lewis came up with a nickel-zinc battery that promises longer life and twice the range of the lead-acid counterpart. Lewis researchers built a prototype battery and installed it in an Otis P-500 electric utility van, using only the battery space already available and allowing battery weight equal to that of the van's conventional lead-acid battery.

In initial tests, the nickel-zinc battery delivered 190 stop-and-go driving cycles per charge, compared with 99 for the lead-acid battery. At a constant speed of 20 miles (32.2 km) per hour—a test speed, not the ultimate expected—the nickel-zinc battery gave the van 55 miles (88.5 km) on a single charge while the lead-acid battery yielded less than 30 miles (48.3 km), or about the distance a golf cart goes between recharges depending on how many times you hook your ball into the rough.

Lewis is continuing research aimed at improving the nickel-zinc battery's performance, life, and competitive cost. The U.S. postal service already has some 450 electric vans, and plans a large-scale expansion utilizing longer-range batteries.

NASA researchers feel that a nickel-zinc battery, producible within five years, could drive a car 120 miles (193.4 km) at an average speed of 40 miles (64.4 km) per hour on a single charge—exceeding the predicted requirement for a viable urban vehicle that would satisfy the present needs of 99 percent of all inner-city travel.

A spinoff with economic potential, because of very wide applicability, is a NASA-developed anticorrosion coating. Because of exposure to salt spray, coastal or ocean structures—bridges, ships, oil rigs, and pipelines, for example—require more corrosion protection than is needed inland. One study showed that a corrosion coating with a twenty-five-year life at an inland location was good for only four to six years in coastal areas. The goal is to find a longer-lasting, single coating to counter the rising cost of applying a second coat.

NASA-Goddard developed a zinc-rich coating in a special solution that gives longer life and has superior adhesion characteristics—so that only a single coat is required. Unlike conventional coatings, the NASA compound is easy to mix and it also costs less. Thus, the new coating offers cost advantages in materials, work hours per application, and fewer applications over a given time span.

Heat resistant paint for spacecraft was used on this racing car.

In Philadelphia the coating has been applied to sample sections of the Frankford Elevated System's steel support structure. On the West Coast, it is being tested on facilities of the Pillar Point Satellite Tracking Station, Pillar Point, California, and on segments of the Golden Gate Bridge. It is also undergoing evaluation by the Vermont Department of Highways as an undercoating to protect road equipment against deicing salts.

NASA-Lewis procedures have been used in testing a variety of structures and systems, ranging from nuclear reactors and power-generating equipment to tractors and plows.

Another transportation-related example involves production of snowmobiles. Deere and Company at Moline, Illinois, used NASA technology as a basis for selecting better aluminum alloys and improving quality control procedures to reduce the chance of failure in high-speed rotary components of snowmobiles.

ELDEC Corporation of Lynwood, Washington, built a weight-recording system for logging trucks based on electronic technology the company acquired as a subcontractor on space programs such as Apollo and the Saturn launch vehicle. The company employed its space-derived expertise to develop a computerized weight-and-balance system for Lockheed's TriStar jetliner. ELDEC then adapted the airliner system to a similar product for use on logging trucks. Electronic equipment computes tractor weight, trailer weight, and overall gross weight, and this information is presented to the driver by an instrument in the cab. The system costs $2,000 but it pays for itself in a single year. It allows operators to use a truck's hauling capacity more efficiently since the load can be maximized without exceeding legal weight limits for highway travel. Approximately four thousand logging trucks now use the system.

[76]

NASA aircraft-icing research has been applied to expand the utility of the big flying-crane helicopter built by the Sikorsky Aircraft Division. Sikorsky wanted to adapt the Skycrane, used in both military and commercial service, to lift heavy external loads in areas where icing conditions occur; ice buildup around the engine air inlets caused the major problem.

NASA-Lewis has a special wind tunnel for injecting supercooled water droplets into the wind thereby simulating a natural icing cloud and observing how ice builds up on various shaped surfaces. From Lewis, Sikorsky engineers obtained information that optimized the design of the inlet anti-ice system. The resulting design proved to be an effective anti-icing modification for the flying crane. Sikorsky is also using additional Lewis Icing Research Tunnel data in its development of a new VTOL (vertical takeoff and landing) aircraft.

SPORTS AND
RECREATION BENEFITS

A spinoff from NASA's space technology helped an expedition climb the world's tallest mountain and it also contributes to a variety of new products for sports and recreation.

On October 8, 1976, climbers Chris Chandler and Bob Cormack battled freezing cold and hundred-mile-an-hour (160.9-kmph) winds to reach the 29,028-foot (8,848-m) summit of Mount Everest in the Nepalese Himalayas.

Chandler and Cormack were members of the American Bicentennial Everest Expedition, which included twelve climbers and some five hundred porters. Only Chandler and Cormack made it to the top; a frozen oxygen regulator forced their Sherpa guide, Ang Phurba, to turn back in the last 1,000 feet (300 m).

The climbers' skill and courage were the main elements of this triumph, but NASA technology played an important supporting role. The transfer from space technology was the oxygen bottle, originally developed as solid rocket propellant tanks at NASA-Lewis.

In order to sustain human life at elevations above 23,000 feet (7,010 m), climbers must breathe oxygen full time—even while sleeping. Among the 40,000 pounds (18,140 kg) of supplies hauled 140 miles (225.3 km) from Katmandu, Nepal, to Mount Everest were 200 oxygen bottles of special design. The individual bottle is an aluminum cylinder overwrapped with reinforcing fiberglass filaments, and each bottle is wrapped with 1,670 miles (2,688 km) of filament three times finer than human hair. This type of construction reduces weight while providing a stronger cylinder. The extra strength permits higher air pressures, or more oxygen in the same volume. Compared with steel cylinders used on previous expeditions, the Luxfer-Compositek bottles—which, incidentally, were filled by NASA's Johnson Space Center—contain approximately twice as much oxygen although they weigh almost 20 percent less.

The weight and air volume advantages of the new bottles reduced the number of cylinders needed and reduced the overall breathing-system weight requirement by about half. This enabled the porters, to whom every ounce counts, to carry more of the vital equipment needed at the high-altitude camps.

The space technology bottles were particularly important in the assault on the summit, which started at an elevation of 27,450 feet (8,467 m). At this level, climbers can carry only 35 pounds (15.9 kg). On previous expeditions, the weight of two cylinders—an active and a spare—made up the bulk of the weight allowance. The new bottles saved Chandler and Cormack 5.5 pounds (2.5 kg) each. Additionally, the greater air volume of the new bottle allowed them to drop off the spare at the base of the summit for pickup on their return, lightening the load for the final climb. Thus, space technology made a significant contribution to the success of the American Bicentennial Everest Expedition.

The Everest application is one example of many technology transfers to sports and recreation. A representative sampling follows.

NASA technology used in developing protective clothing for astronauts is finding new application in a line of outdoor gear produced by Comfort Products of Aspen, Colorado. The company supplied leading ski boot manufacturers with built-in rechargeable electric foot-warmers, the design of which was borrowed from Apollo heating element circuitry. ThermaFlex, a woven mesh material designed to allow air to flow under and around an astronaut's feet, has a number of applications. Among them are the Procover "stay-dry" bicycle seat and the Profoot Insole, for more comfortable athletic and outdoor footwear.

Among a number of solar energy tests being jointly conducted by NASA's Lewis Research Center and the Department of Energy are a sun-powered refrigerator and a back-pack mounted power supply for radios. Both use solar cells, spacecraft power sources that convert the sun's energy into electricity. The refrigerator, which has potential utility for outdoor campers, is in operation at a trail construction camp in Isle Royale National Park, a remote wilderness in Lake Superior where electricity is available only at park headquarters. Trail maintenance crews working in the back country get food supplies only once weekly. With refrigeration, they can enjoy a more varied and nutritious diet. Solar cells provide power to run the refrigerator and to charge its batteries for an alternate power supply when the sun is not available.

At the request of Inyo National Forest personnel, the NASA-Lewis scientists also developed a back-pack system. The lightweight solar cell pack charges batteries for portable two-way radios used by trail guards, who are on patrol for as much as two weeks at a time. Guards want continuous communication with the district station, but ordinary battery capacity precludes such operation. With the solar cell power supply, guards can use their radios twenty-four hours a day.

Space age technology spinoffs, whether transferred to America's benefit in the national parks, in medicine, or in nonpersonal areas such as commerce and industry, are a billion dollar-plus advantage to the nation. In time they will surely increase tenfold and benefit the rest of the world, too.

SOURCES OF
ADDITIONAL INFORMATION

BOOKS TO CONSULT

Colby, C. B. *Space Age Spinoffs*. New York: Coward, McCann & Geoghegan, 1972.

Ordway, F. I., III, Adams, C. C., and Sharpe, M. R., Jr. *Dividends from Space*. New York: Thomas Y. Crowell, 1971.

Taylor, L. B., Jr. *Gifts from Space*. New York: John Day, 1977.

PAMPHLETS TO CONSULT

Landsat: NASA Earth Resources Satellite. General Electric Company, Space Division, Valley Forge Space Center, P.O. Box 8555, Philadelphia, Pa. 19101, 1975.

NASA Tech Briefs. National Aeronautics and Space Administration, Director, Technology Utilization Office, P.O. Box 8757, Baltimore/Washington International Airport, Md. 21240 (published quarterly since spring 1976).

NASA Tech House. National Aeronautics and Space Administration, Washington, D.C. 20546, U.S. Government Printing Office, 1977.

New Horizons. National Aeronautics and Space Administration, Washington, D.C. 20546, U.S. Government Printing Office, 1975.

Spinoff 1978, An Annual Report (also, *Spinoff 1977* and *Spinoff 1976*). James J. Haggerty, National Aeronautics and Space Administration, Washington, D.C. 20546, U.S. Government Printing Office.

For further information about the NASA Technology Spinoff Network write the Technology Utilization Officer at your nearest NASA Field Center.

NASA FIELD CENTERS:
Ames Research Center
National Aeronautics & Space Administration
Moffett Field, Calif. 90435

Hugh L. Dryden Flight Research Center
National Aeronautics & Space Administration
P.O. Box 273
Edwards, Calif. 93523

Goddard Space Flight Center
National Aeronautics & Space Administration
Greenbelt, Md. 20771

Lyndon B. Johnson Space Center
National Aeronautics & Space Administration
Houston, Tex. 77058

John F. Kennedy Space Center
National Aeronautics & Space Administration
Kennedy Space Center, Fla. 32899

Langley Research Center
National Aeronautics & Space Administration
Langley Station
Hampton, Va. 23655

Lewis Research Center
National Aeronautics & Space Administration
21000 Brookpark Road
Cleveland, Ohio 44135

George C. Marshall Space Flight Center
National Aeronautics & Space Administration
Marshall Space Flight Center, Ala. 35812

NASA Jet Propulsion Laboratory
4800 Oak Grove Drive
Pasadena, Calif. 91103

Wallops Flight Center
National Aeronautics & Space Administration
Wallops Island, Va. 23337

Educators may receive additional information on NASA publications, films, and services by writing to the Education Office serving their state:

IF YOU LIVE IN:	WRITE TO EDUCATION OFFICE AT:
Alaska	NASA Ames Research Center
Arizona	Moffet Field, California 94035
California	
Hawaii	
Idaho	
Montana	
Nevada	
Oregon	
Utah	
Washington	
Wyoming	
Alabama	NASA George C. Marshall Space Flight Center
Arkansas	Marshall Space Flight Center
Iowa	Alabama 35812
Louisiana	
Mississippi	
Missouri	
Tennessee	
Connecticut *	NASA Goddard Space Flight Center
Delaware	Greenbelt, Maryland 20771
District of Columbia	

Maine *
Maryland
Massachusetts *
New Hampshire *
New Jersey
New York *
Pennsylvania
Rhode Island *
Vermont *

Florida	NASA John F. Kennedy Space Center
Georgia	Kennedy Space Center
Puerto Rico	Florida 32899
Virgin Islands	
Kentucky	NASA Langley Research Center
North Carolina	Langley Station
South Carolina	Hampton, Virginia 23365
Virginia	
West Virginia	
Illinois	NASA Lewis Research Center
Indiana	21000 Brookpark Road
Michigan	Cleveland, Ohio 44135
Minnesota	
Ohio	
Wisconsin	
Colorado	NASA Lyndon B. Johnson Space Center
Kansas	Houston, Texas 77058
Nebraska	
New Mexico	
North Dakota	
Oklahoma	
South Dakota	
Texas	

* For film loans, persons in these states should
write to:
National Audiovisual Center
General Services Administration
Washington, D.C. 20409

INDEX